THE SHED

nut

by debbie tucker green

nut

by debbie tucker green

CAST

Elayne **Nadine Marshall**
Aimee **Sophie Stanton**
Devon **Anthony Welsh**
Trey **Tobi Adetunji** or **Zac Fitzgerald** or **Jayden Fowora-Knight**
Ex-Wife **Sharlene Whyte**
Ex-Husband **Gershwyn Eustache Jr**

Director **debbie tucker green**
Designer **Lisa Marie Hall**
Lighting Designer **Tim Mitchell**
Movement **Polly Bennett**
Music **Matthew Scott**
Sound Designer **Emma Laxton**
Company Voice Work **Jeannette Nelson**

Production Manager **Tariq Hussain**
Staff Director **Ng Choon Ping**
Stage Manager **Nik Haffenden**
Deputy Stage Manager **Charlotte Padgham**
Assistant Stage Manager **Sophie Bowman**
Costume Supervisor **Lucy Walshaw**
Props Supervisor **Rebecca Johnston**
Assistant to the Lighting Designer **Kate Greaves**
Project Draughting **Tom Springett**
Casting **Charlotte Bevan**
Production Photographer **Stephen Cummiskey**

WORLD PREMIERE
The Shed
30 October to 5 December 2013

LENGTH
About 75 minutes. (There is no interval. Please check with front-of-house staff for accurate timings).

The National's workshops are responsible for, on this production: Costume; Props & furniture; Scenic construction; Scenic lighting; Scenic painting; Wigs, hair and make-up

PRODUCTION CREDITS
With thanks to Juliet Messenger; Marian Doyle; Natasha Vincent.

nut poster image: **Raw Creative**
Programme pages design:
Joel Rajwadi

The National Theatre wishes to acknowledge its partner **National Angels Limited**

ACCESS
Copies of this cast list, in braille or large print, are available from the Shed Box Offiice.

Audio-described performance: Saturday 16 November at 3.30pm (Touch Tour at 2.15pm).

Captioned performance: Tuesday 26 November at 8pm.

SHOP
Playtexts of debbie tucker green's work are on sale in the National Theatre Bookshop in the main foyer. Open Mon to Sat, 9.30am to 10.45pm; Sun 12pm to 6pm.
shop.nationaltheatre.org.uk

The Shed Partner

Neptune Investment Management
We have been working with the National Theatre since 2009, and are delighted to continue our support as The Shed Partner. As a young, dynamic and innovative investment management company, our partnership with The Shed is a natural collaboration as a space that will celebrate new theatre that is original, ambitious and unexpected.

theshedtheatre.co.uk/aboutus

TOBI ADETUNJI
Trey
Tobi Adetunji trains at Freedom Academy. *nut* is his professional theatre debut.

GERSHYN EUSTACHE JNR
Ex-Husband
Gershwyn Eustache Jnr trained at Identity Drama School.
His work in **theatre** includes: *Macbeth on Film* (Globe); *As You Like It* (Lion and the Unicorn); *Romeo and Juliet* (UK tour); *The Malcontent* (White Bear); *Someone to Blame* (Theatre503); and *Closer* (Arcola).
TV includes: *Run* and *VIP*.
Films include: *second coming*, *Starred Up* and *Fat Cat*.

ZAC FITZGERALD
Trey
Zac Fitzgerald trains at ACT 2 Drama. *nut* is his professional theatre debut.

JAYDEN FOWORA-KNIGHT
Trey
Jayden Fowora-Knight trains at Sylvia Young Theatre School.
His work in **theatre** includes: *The Bodyguard* in the West End.

NADINE MARSHALL
Elayne
Nadine Marshall trained at Rose Bruford.
Her work in **theatre** includes: *Henry VIII*, *Oroonoko* and *The Spanish Tragedy* (RSC); *Random* (Royal Court); *Born Bad* (Hampstead); *The Last Valentine* (Almeida); and *Shoot to Win* (Theatre Royal, Stratford East).
TV includes: *Old Jack's Boat* (series 1 & 2), *The Spa*, *The Gates*, *random* (Black International Film Festival/MVSA award winner, Best Actress; BAFTA, Best Actress nomination), *Rick and Peter*, *Excluded*, *The Shadow Line*, *Casualty*, *Criminal Justice*, *The Commander*, *Jackanory*, *The Smoking Room*.
Film includes: *second coming*, *Love at First Sight*, *heat*, *It's a Free World*, *Shish* and *Club le Monde*.
Radio: *Martin Beck*, *My Boy*, *No1 Ladies Detective Agency*, *gone*, *Bad Faith*, *The Color Purple*, *From Lagos with Love*, *Dombey and Son*, *The Thebans*, and *Measure for Measure*.

SOPHIE STANTON
Aimee
Sophie Stanton trained at RADA.
Her work in **theatre** includes: *England People Very Nice* and *Market Boy* (National); *Slaughter City* (RSC); *Ding Dong the Wicked* (Royal Court); *Knot of the Heart*, *Cloud Nine*, and *Dying for It* (Almeida); *Beautiful Thing* (Sound); *Cariad* (Tristan Bates); *A Collier's Friday Night* (Hampstead); *Bright* (Soho); *Crossing the Equator* and *Backstroke in a Crowded Pool* (Bush); *Breezeblock Park* (Liverpool Playhouse); *She Stoops to Conquer* (New Kent Opera); *Hindle Wakes*, *Love's Labour's Lost* (Royal Exchange)
TV: *My Mad Fat Diary 2*, *The Smoke*, *New Tricks*, *Mayday*, *The Silent and*

the Damned, EastEnders, One Night, Ashes to Ashes, Hunter, Wallander, Whitechapel, Silent Witness, The Brief, The Vice, Girl's Night, Tough Love, The Wilsons, Black Books, The Mayor of Casterbridge, Gimme Gimme Gimme, Plastic Man, Prime Suspect, Shine On Harvey Moon.
Film includes: How I Live Now, Cheerful Weather for the Wedding, Grow Your Own, Beautiful Thing and Shadowlands.

ANTHONY WELSH
Devon
Anthony Welsh trained at LAMDA.
His work in **theatre** includes: Blackta and The Brothers Size (also on tour) (Young Vic); Sucker Punch (Royal Court); Pornography (Tricycle; tour); and Precious Little Talent and Lower Ninth (West End).
TV includes: Secrets and Words, Life's Too Short, and Top Boy.
Films include: second coming, Starred Up, Dirty Money, My Brother The Devil, Comes a Bright Day, Home and Red Tails.
Radio: Carnival, Hello Mum, The Interrogation and David and Goliath

SHARLENE WHYTE
Ex-Wife
Sharlene Whyte trained at RADA.
Her work in **theatre** includes: Julius Caesar (RSC); born bad (Hampstead); Arabian Nights (Young Vic); Three Birds (Gate); Treasure Island (West End).
TV includes: Run, Jonathan Creek, Waterloo Road, Coronation Street, Secrets and Words, Spooks, and Undisclosed.
Film includes: second coming.
Radio: to swallow and A Million Different People.

debbie tucker green
Writer/Director
Theatre includes: truth and reconciliation, random, stoning mary (Royal Court); generations (Young Vic); trade (RSC), born bad (Hampstead); dirty butterfly (Soho).
Television and **film** includes: second coming (feature film), random, heat (short film).
Radio includes: gone, random, handprint, to swallow, freefall.
Directing includes: second coming (feature film), truth and reconciliation (play), random (film), heat (short film), gone, random (radio).
Awards: Olivier, Most Promising Newcomer for born bad 2004; OBIE for born bad New York Soho Rep production 2011; BAFTA for Best Single Drama 2012 for random film; Black International Film/MVSA award Best UK Film for random 2011.

LISA MARIE HALL
Designer
Training: National Film & TV School (MA Film Design).
Theatre: truth and reconciliation.
Production Design for film: second coming, Still Life, Somers Town.
Production Design for TV: What Remains, Holy Flying Circus, random, This Is England '86, New Town.
She designed the Great Glass Elevator for the film Charlie & the Chocolate Factory. **lisamariehall.com**

TIM MITCHELL
Lighting Designer

Tim Mitchell is an Associate Lighting Designer for the RSC and Chichester Festival Theatre.

Productions for the National: *Noises Off, The Red Balloon* and *The Alchemist.*

Other theatre: *The Winslow Boy* (Old Vic); *Kiss Me Kate* (Old Vic/Chichester); *A Chorus of Disapproval* (West End); *My Fair Lady* (Sheffield); *Singin' in the Rain* (Olivier nomination Best Musical Revival, West End/Chichester); *The Sound of Music, Crazy For You* (West End/Regent's Park); *Dirty Dancing* (West End/International); *Written on the Heart* (West End/RSC); *The Lion, The Witch and The Wardrobe* (Kensington); *Goodnight Mr. Tom* (West End/UK Tour); *Yes Prime Minister* (West End/UK Tour/Chichester); *A Human Being Died That Night* (Hampstead); *The Turn of The Screw* (Almeida); *Rosencrantz and Guildenstern Are Dead* (West End/Chichester); *Richard II, The Orphan of Zhao, The City Madam* (RSC); *Forests* (Birmingham Rep); *Dr. Faustus* (West Yorkshire Playhouse); *The Play What I Wrote* (Broadway/West End); *Merrily We Roll Along* (Donmar); *Hamlet* (Japan/Sadler's Wells).

POLLY BENNETT
Movement

Training: Royal Central School of Speech and Drama; National Youth Theatre

Theatre: NT: *nut*; RSC: Resident Movement Practitioner, *A Mad World My Masters, A Life of Galileo* (Assistant), *'Tis a Pity She's a Whore* (Workshop) **Opera**: *Acis and Galatea*. **On tour**: *Dunsinane*

Other theatre: *Hysteria, Pope Joan, The People of the Town, Lobsters, Short and Stark, The Wind in the Willows, Mudlarks, Les Misérables, Celebrity Night at Café Red, Don Juan Comes Back from the War, The Folk Contraption, The Lights, The Man with the Luggage, Sum Zero, A Midsummer Night's Dream, She Stoops to Conquer, S'warm, Love, Question Mark, Fastburn, Normal, Precious Little Talent.*

TV: *Fazer's Urban Symphony, The Coronation Concerts* (BBC) Polly Bennett was Movement Assistant on London 2012 Opening Ceremony and Mass Movement on the Closing Ceremony and Paralympic Opening Ceremony. She is Mass Choreographer on the Sochi Winter Olympics Opening Ceremony.

MATTHEW SCOTT
Music

Theatre credits include: over 25 productions for the National Theatre, most recently *The Doctor's Dilemma*.

Other recent theatre includes: *Arturo Ui, The Deep Blue Sea* and *Rattigan's Nijinsky* (Chichester/West End); *Private Lives* (West End/Broadway); and *The Hypochondriac* (Almeida). Recent work for children: *Horrible Histories, George's Marvellous Medicine* and *Horrible Science*. **TV** includes: *Middlemarch, Bedtime, Drop the Dead Donkey, Sex 'n' Death, Lord of Misrule, King Leek, Crossing the Floor, Mrs Bradley's Mysteries* and *Underworld*.

Films include: *The Landgirls, The Feast of July* and *King Girl*.
Matthew Scott trained at the Guildhall School and City University London followed by studies in Berlin and New York where he worked as Music Assistant to Lotte Lenya. He has written music for many plays including premieres by Alan Bennett, Richard Bean, Harold Pinter, Mark Ravenhill, and Howard Barker. He was a member of cult systems band The Lost Jockey, and has produced Trans Global Underground, Antony and the Johnstons and Martha Wainwright. His orchestral version of 'Sergeant Pepper's Lonely Hearts Club Band' was premiered by the London Sinfonietta at the Milan Festival in 2007 sung by Jarvis Cocker, Marianne Faithfull and others; that year he also appeared with Faithless in Moscow. Matthew Scott is Head of Music at the NT, an Associate of Chichester Festival Theatre and Honorary Vice President of the Chichester City Band.

EMMA LAXTON
Sound Designer
Emma Laxton's work in **theatre** includes: *All My Sons, A Doll's House, Three Birds, The Accrington Pals, Lady Windermere's Fan* (Royal Exchange, Manchester); *Much Ado About Nothing* (Old Vic), *The Promise, Berenice, The Physicists, Making Noise Quietly, The Recruiting Officer* (Donmar); *The Westbridge, The Heretic, Off the Endz, Tusk Tusk, Faces in the Crowd, Gone Too Far, Catch, Scenes from the Back of Beyond, Woman and Scarecrow, The World's Biggest Diamond, Incomplete and Random Acts of Kindness, Bone, The Weather, Bear Hug, Terrorism, Food Chain* (Royal Court); *That Face* (West End/Royal Court); *My Name Is Rachel Corrie* (West End/New York/Edinburgh Festival/Royal Court); *The Arrest of Ai Weiwei, Lay Down Your Cross, Blue Heart Afternoon* (Hampstead); *OMG* (Sadler's Wells/The Place/Company of Angels); *There are Mountains* (Clean Break/HMP Askham Grange); *You Can Still Make A Killing* (Southwark Playhouse); *The Sacred Flame* (ETT); *Much Ado About Nothing, Precious Little Talent* (West End); *Where's My Seat, Like A Fishbone, The Whisky Taster, If There Is I Haven't Found It Yet* (Bush); *Men Should Weep* (National Theatre); *Sisters* (Sheffield Crucible).

NG CHOON PING
Staff Director
Training: Central School of Speech and Drama, York University.
Awards: Royal Exchange Hodgkiss Award for Young Directors.
Directing: *Golden Child, Snap, Armed Forces Day, Yolk, The Matchmakers, Pure O.*
Assistant Directing: *Chimerica, Someone to Blame, Constance.*
Shakespeare's Globe Text Associate: *King Lear, Taming of the Shrew, Henry VI.*

While you're here

EAT AND DRINK Find restaurants, cafés and bars throughout the National Theatre.

SHOP Playtexts, programmes, posters, books, recordings, gifts and merchandise. Mon to Sat, 9.30am to 10.45pm; Sun 12 noon to 6pm.

GO BACKSTAGE Daily tours. 75 minutes, £8.50/£7.50. Details from the Information Desk.

BROWSE FREE EXHIBITIONS Photographic, fine art and design. All year round.

JOIN: more information on membership schemes from the Information Desk.

Your National Theatre

The National Theatre opened here in 1976 and each year stages more than 20 productions, from brand new plays to world classics – on the South Bank, in the West End and on tour. But the work isn't just on the stage.

NT LEARNING enables people of all ages to discover the excitement of theatre-making. **NATIONAL THEATRE LIVE** broadcasts the best of British theatre live to cinemas across the globe. There are costumes and props for **HIRE**; **PLATFORM** talks and interviews; an **ARCHIVE** of the NT's history; **DIGITAL** resources to explore at any time and in any place.

It's all here:
nationaltheatre.org.uk

NTFuture
transforming the National Theatre of Great Britain

The Shed is our temporary theatre while the Cottesloe is closed as part of the £70 million NT Future redevelopment project. The Cottesloe will reopen as the Dorfman Theatre in Spring 2014. Will you support NT Future with a donation to help us reach our target? To thank you, we could name a seat for you in the Dorfman Theatre, engrave a paving stone, or include your name on our Supporters Mural. Find out more **nationaltheatre.org.uk/ntfuture**

Chairman of the NT Board **John Makinson**
Director of the National Theatre **Nicholas Hytner**
Executive Director **Nick Starr**
Chief Operating Officer **Lisa Burger**
Deputy Executive Director **Kate Horton**

nationaltheatre.org.uk

National Theatre

Supported using public funding by
ARTS COUNCIL ENGLAND

nut

debbie tucker green

Characters

ELAYNE, *Black female*
AIMEE, *White female*
DEVON, *Black male*
TREY, *Black boy*
EX-WIFE, *Black, younger sister of Elayne*
EX-HUSBAND, *Tyrone, Black*
DAUGHTER, *Maya, approximately eleven years old (heard
    from offstage only)*

Time: Now.

A forward slash (/) marks where dialogue starts to overlap.

*Names appearing without dialogue indicate an active silence
between those characters.*

Words in (brackets) are intention only and not to be spoken.

*This text went to press before the end of rehearsals and so may
differ slightly from the play as performed.*

ACT ONE

Scene One

In ELAYNE*'s place.*

ELAYNE	It would start with something bout how I am.
AIMEE	Original.
ELAYNE	Not no shit about how people think I am but how I (am) how I really / am.
AIMEE	I'd write / it.
ELAYNE	Wouldn't trust you to write it I'd write it – have something / prepared.
AIMEE	You can't write it – y'not meant to write / it.
ELAYNE	I'd write / it.
AIMEE	Someone else is meant to write it –
ELAYNE	someone / who?
AIMEE	someone else is meant to say the nice somethings that's / the (point) –
ELAYNE	someone / who?
AIMEE	that's the point, writin your own is wrong – writin your own is arrogant.
ELAYNE	I'd be being accurate.
AIMEE	Your version a accurate which is arrogant.
	I'd get it right.
ELAYNE	Wouldn't trust you to get it right, toldju.
AIMEE	I'd get the tone right – get the feel, work the crowd or whoever shows up – you'd just write the good bits / about –

ELAYNE   The point is to write the good bits no one
             knows about

AIMEE   can't be that good if no one don't know bout
             them.

ELAYNE   Discreetly good.

AIMEE   'Discreetly good'?

ELAYNE   You're only good when people are watchin.

AIMEE   If no one's there then there is no point – when
             no one's there you can just be yourself –

ELAYNE   which is what?

AIMEE   I know me. And you aint no / angel.

ELAYNE   I'm good whether you watchin or not – not
             waitin on no audience.

AIMEE   Wouldn't sit there and watch.

ELAYNE   Might learn something.

AIMEE   Not from you.
             I'd write your eulogy and people / would –

ELAYNE   You're not writing mine not writing on / mine.

AIMEE   people would remember, people would recall
             and regret –

ELAYNE   don't want no one's regrets don't want no
             regrets – this is / why –

AIMEE   or if not regrets then – I'd write somethin /
             that –

ELAYNE   *this* is why you're not getting nowhere near / it.

AIMEE   you write it people'll be like – 'who does she
             think she is?'

ELAYNE   Nowhere / near.

AIMEE   'Who the fuck does she think she is?'

ELAYNE   Right.

AIMEE	You don't want that to be their last / impression of –
ELAYNE	They / won't.
AIMEE	their last impression of you.
ELAYNE	They wouldn't know who wrote what if I wrote it – they'd juss hear the words –
AIMEE	they'd / know.
ELAYNE	hear the words and be too busy / bein sad –
AIMEE	They'd know cos I'd tellem. What bits I did and what bits I didn't. I'd leave a taste, leave an odour somethin that'll linger longer than the service – an emotional stain –
ELAYNE	my people would smell your bullshit –
AIMEE	that's how I'd write your / eulogy.
ELAYNE	they'd know iss not bout me and embarrass you, their impression of me intact, solid amongst your written / shit.
AIMEE	I'd be honest boutchu not harsh – not too harsh, but / honest.
ELAYNE	They'd know and you wouldn't be invited –
AIMEE	you wouldn't know if I'd be there
ELAYNE	getchu barred.
AIMEE	By who? You gonna have bouncers on the doors-of-your-demise? Even more – see – even more bout 'Who the fuck she think she is with security?'
ELAYNE	Get it written in you ent got no entry… People like you wouldn't be invited.
AIMEE	Like me who?
ELAYNE	Like / you.
AIMEE	Who am I like?

ELAYNE	(*quietly*) …Y'not like no one I know.
AIMEE	What?
ELAYNE	Y'not like no one I / know.
AIMEE	I aint like no one you know, that's right. I'm unique. Who you know? Who you invitin? Who'd you know to invite even?
	Beat.
	You'd want me there.
ELAYNE	…You'd have to do the inviting –
AIMEE	what?
ELAYNE	…You'd have to do the inviting –
AIMEE	(so) you want me to / do that.
ELAYNE	you'd do the contacting –
AIMEE	not allowed in not allowed to say nothing not allowed to write nuthin but have to do the donkey / work?
ELAYNE	Someone gotta do the –
AIMEE	(*dry*) write a / list.
ELAYNE	I can't do the – if I'm / not –
AIMEE	Get someone else to do it.
ELAYNE	I'm tellin you.
AIMEE	Get someone else to contact your few / friends.
ELAYNE	I'm tellin you.
AIMEE	I'm tellin you no.
ELAYNE	I'm askin.
	…You'd do it.
	Beat.

AIMEE	Who'd you invite?
ELAYNE	
AIMEE	Who'd you have there – who've you got to come?
ELAYNE	…Everybody I know.
AIMEE	Which is?
ELAYNE	Just be everybody / I know.
AIMEE	Thass a cupful.
ELAYNE	There's / plenty.
AIMEE	Hire half the pews only need part of the place – short and sweet – do a double deal – one side someone else who don't know no one – got no one to invite and the other side be your cupful of few / friends.
ELAYNE	You don't know my people –
AIMEE	know there's not much people to know, know there aint hardly any to know and out of the few that there is, only / a couple –
ELAYNE	you don't / know –
AIMEE	a couple probably worth knowing. I'll do your invites only take me bout ten minutes – service only be about twenty – me, the Pastor and your few that turn up.
ELAYNE	They'll turn up.
AIMEE	Y'think?
ELAYNE	You'll be outside but they'll turn up and get in.
AIMEE	Get in cos it's half empty and you wouldn't know who was comin if you hadn't invited them and how'd you know I wouldn't fuck it up?
ELAYNE	You won't fuck it up – a five year / old –

AIMEE	Might fuck it up on / purpose.
ELAYNE	a five year old couldn't fuck that up so I think you do got the ability to stick a invite in a envelope and a name on a invite and an address on the front.
AIMEE	…With a stamp.
ELAYNE	(*dry*) With a stamp yes. See. You already know what you doin.
AIMEE	
ELAYNE	…And I'd leave a list –
AIMEE	knew you couldn't leave it / alone.
ELAYNE	leave a list of instructions –
AIMEE	I wouldn't read / it.
ELAYNE	yeh you would – a little short something – just to / y'know –
AIMEE	I wouldn't read / it.
ELAYNE	just so you – something to guide you. Just in case any fuck-upery is tempted to take over. And you would read it cos you couldn't help yourself can't help yourself, all curious and interested and all up in my business before my body's even cold – you'd read it.
AIMEE	…How long a list?
ELAYNE	Long enough.
AIMEE	How long a / list?
ELAYNE	Long enough.
	Beat.
AIMEE	…Make sure you type it then cos I can't read your shit scribble –
ELAYNE	you can't read
AIMEE	I don't bother with your mess on a page

ELAYNE   do my long words confuse yer?

AIMEE   Reading your shit aint worth the effort. And I
                wouldn't sit there and try.

                Beat.
                Beat.

ELAYNE   …What would you have writ?
                What would you have written in yours?

                Beat.

AIMEE   '…Brilliant.'

ELAYNE
AIMEE

AIMEE   Thass it. 'Brilliant.'

ELAYNE   One word?

AIMEE   One word.

ELAYNE   One / word?

AIMEE   One word, no lists, no instructions.
                I was. It was. I will be remembered as. Done.
                Brilliant.

ELAYNE   …'Brilliant.'

AIMEE   'Brilliant.'

ELAYNE   Thass not no eulogy, that's a piss take.

AIMEE   They'd have to shift my service to a bigger
                venue, have your security explaining to my
                people a bigger venue's a necessity cos there'd
                be so many people turning up – and the people
                won't be surprised and they'll be willin and the
                overspill won't be able to get in but will be
                cool. Do a memorial days after – weeks after.
                Two. Have them video screens up outside and
                outside speakers for the outside people and
                crash barriers so they don't get crushed.
                They'll be standing street-side, still and solemn
                and listening and payin their / respects.

ELAYNE   Everybody who?

AIMEE   Half of the everybody I know will be that
                much, weepin and wailing and recalling how
                'brilliant' I / was.

ELAYNE   Cos *that's* not arrogant at / all.

AIMEE   There's a difference between me bein
                arrogant and me bein honest. I'm honest –
                bein honest – playin humble aint helpful,
                those with their own insecurities will take my
                honesty as arrogance, my confidence as a
                threat – but I can't help their issues when all
                I'm bein is / myself.

ELAYNE   I juss think you're arrogant.

AIMEE   As I have explained –

ELAYNE   ignorant and arrogant and you bein you is not
                'good' as you have said –

AIMEE   your / insecurities –

ELAYNE   and I'm not feelin no 'threat' from your /
                'arrogance'.

AIMEE   I said confidence threatens you need to /
                listen better.

ELAYNE   And I ent got no insecurities and you couldn't
                threaten me and your 'arrogance' is just
                annoyin and you don't know nuff of nobody
                to fill up a service twice and a memorial on
                top of that. Be you, security, a bag of empty
                pews and a pastor bored reading out your one
                word eulogy.

                Beat.

AIMEE   …Know more people than you.

ELAYNE   Least I'd know the people I'd be inviting –
                you just have the waifs and strays thatchu
                pick / up.

AIMEE   Friends.

ELAYNE   They aint friends.

AIMEE   I've *got* friends and you aint doin your
           inviting to yours according to you are yer?
           That'll be down to me according to you and
           your 'instructions', so you don't know who
           the few I'd scrape together to get to go to
           yours would even / be.

ELAYNE   You go before I do I would.

AIMEE   You be the first.

ELAYNE   No.

AIMEE   You be the first to go by a mile.

ELAYNE   No I won't.

AIMEE   Really.

ELAYNE   (*dry*) …'Brilliant.'

AIMEE   Carved in. Deep. On the headstone and on the
           coffin –

ELAYNE   they don't engrave the coffin

AIMEE   mine would be. Different. See. Unique

ELAYNE   stupid.

AIMEE   Unique.

           Beat.

ELAYNE   I wouldn't go.

AIMEE   You wouldn't get in.

ELAYNE   I wouldn't go to yours if I / could.

AIMEE   Not invited.

ELAYNE   I'm on the list – written myself on the list.
           Be / quiet.

AIMEE   You wouldn't be writing it –

ELAYNE	I'm in.
AIMEE	Wouldn't want you to write it –
ELAYNE	I'm in.
AIMEE	You're / not.
ELAYNE	I'm in I'm in. I'm in. If I was goin.

ELAYNE   Half your people wouldn't even know why they were there – half your people be there for the freeness and wouldn't know why – wouldn't know you wouldn't wanna know you.

The other half probably turn up on the wrong day. At the wrong place. At the wrong time at the wrong place.

The other half be trying to work out what the fuck 'brilliant' means –

AIMEE   how many halves / you got?

ELAYNE   in relation to you, 'brilliant? Is that it?' is what they'll be askin me, I'll be sayin:
'I don't know,'
'Is that really it?'
they'll ask *again*, and I'll have to respond *again* with a:
'I really dunno what she was thinkin as I said it was shit – told her it was arrogant' –
and amongst the hymning and –

AIMEE   don't want no / hymns.

ELAYNE   *and* crying they'll hold down a small fake smile and say quiet like:
'Glad you said that'
bit guilty they'll whisper to me:
'Glad you brought that arrogant aspect up cos we was thinking the same thing' –
and they'll look in their hymn books / look –

AIMEE   Aint havin no / hymns.

ELAYNE   *look* back at me sayin it as they're pretend
            singing and I'll just turn my face away and
            sing the song and try and say nuthin else.
            'Who the fuck she think she is?'
            is what they'll be pondering during the
            prayers –

AIMEE   aint having no prayers

ELAYNE   good people thinking bad thoughts cos of you
            me keepin an eye on the Pastor,
            'Who the fuck does / she think she is?'

AIMEE   Aint having no prayers

ELAYNE   you need prayers

AIMEE   don't want no / prayers.

ELAYNE   you need prayin for – and Pastor will pass me
            after reading your one word shit and say,
            'She's a bit fuckin arrogant.'

AIMEE
ELAYNE

ELAYNE   I'll write down what I think should be writ
            bout you for your eulogy as an instruction for
            part of your service plan. As a favour.
            Typed.
            It can only help.

            Beat.

AIMEE

AIMEE   Natural causes is how I'm going out.

ELAYNE

AIMEE   Nothing but natural / causes.

ELAYNE   You hope.

AIMEE   You be long gone before that –

ELAYNE   nope.

AIMEE	Yeh you –
ELAYNE	nope
AIMEE	we'll see.
ELAYNE	We / will.

AIMEE   So I'm just letting you know, natural causes.
            I'll go t'bed feelin alright or something, wake
            up – well – *don't* wake up – just be naturally
            caused, eased outta this existence. A hot drink
            the night before, a lay down and a don't get
            up. Nice.

ELAYNE   'Brilliant.'

AIMEE   Till the last drop see – brilliant even at / that.

ELAYNE   I dunno what's more shit, watchin you be you
            or being you.

AIMEE   Being you means not being me, see, a deficit
            there already – before you even started we
            running at a loss.

ELAYNE	Being me is –
AIMEE	what?
ELAYNE	Being me –
AIMEE	what?

AIMEE
ELAYNE

AIMEE	Is what?
ELAYNE	Is…
AIMEE	See my point.

AIMEE
ELAYNE

ELAYNE   (*quietly*) 'Brilliant.'

AIMEE   And you aint that.
               Case. Rested.
               One word. Inscribed deep and careful. Gold
               leafed and everything. Crowd a people oohing
               and aaahing – tears and heartbreak over my
               coffin, alla that and more.
               Thass it. Done. Done and dusted. Nice.

Scene Two

               In ELAYNE*'s place as before.* DEVON *is
               there too.*

DEVON   …If there ent no bell. People get confused.
               It's confusing

AIMEE   if you're stupid.

DEVON   No bell is like no interest. Not interested.
               Don't care – don't wanna / know.

ELAYNE   I don't / care.

AIMEE   She don't wanna know.

ELAYNE   Don't speak for / me.

DEVON   You don't care?

ELAYNE   I don't wanna know.

DEVON   If you had an outward view, a curiosity, a
               natural curiosity like normal people –

ELAYNE   I'm / normal.

DEVON   you would have a bell

AIMEE   bullshit.

DEVON   But by having *no* bell –

ELAYNE   there is a bell –

DEVON	by havin no bell that *works* – and it's not bullshit – is confusing. Says something about you –
ELAYNE	says –
DEVON	says confusion, says you don't give a shit, better to have *no* bell –
ELAYNE	it says the batteries are / dead.
AIMEE	There is / a bell.
DEVON	Than a bell that don't do nothing. Exposes an aspect of you before you've even opened up and met.
AIMEE	Knock.
DEVON	Ring the bell think it's a quiet one –
ELAYNE	knock
DEVON	ring it twice just in case – ring it a third time knowing whoever is in is by now pissed off to the highest – you will not be dropping a knock as well, talk / sense.
AIMEE	Ring it once – don't get shit – knock twice –
ELAYNE	twice is annoying
AIMEE	thass the code – knock it twice just in case the inside person aint heard –
DEVON	confusion.
ELAYNE	Code?
AIMEE	Social code everyone / knows.
ELAYNE	Everybody / who?
AIMEE	First knock is a gentle touch with a hesitation. Like the first and only ring – not bein sure if them thass inside have heard. Second knock you don't give a fuck make your presence felt and let them know that y'still outside cold and wet.

DEVON	See, so you've pissed them off before they're even in.
AIMEE	And if you (ELAYNE) was halfway social you'd know, dunno where you're (DEVON) goin bout three rings – three rings is madness – three rings is formal or legal or looking for you when you shouldn't be looked for – when you don't wanna be found. Bailiff, bills or some other bollocks is a three ring madness –
ELAYNE	(*dry*) code
AIMEE	three rings, don't answer the door – ring it once, knock once, knock twice – everyone's cool. Knows where they're at, flip the combination even but three / times?
DEVON	How many doors do you knock?
AIMEE	Ring knock knock that's my / combo.
DEVON	Not you, her.
ELAYNE	I just knock don't try bells.
DEVON	You don't go / out.
ELAYNE	Bells is the (problem) from you don't even know if they're a workin one why try? Ring it off too long – problem, too short – dilemma. Buzzer, bell or ding dong –
AIMEE	no one you know's got a ding-dong –
DEVON	she don't know no one to / know.
AIMEE	Your kinda people have a half arsed Argos type a / effort.
ELAYNE	Your people y'just shout up at windows for –
AIMEE	not even wired in, battered battery type a / bell.
ELAYNE	chuck an empty can up for – ent worth ringin your people's bells cos they aint gonna be hearin nuthin all sleeping off their night-before-last-night at all hours of the day. (A)

	bell's wasted on your waifs and strays – probably ent even their bells they're sleepin under anyway, somebody else's floor they've crashed / on.
AIMEE	Woolworths.
DEVON	Woolworths done.
AIMEE	That's your bell effort – her old bell effort – so old – yeh Woolworths *is* done – your shit's so old you can't take it back cos the shop don't even exist / no more.
ELAYNE	If I ent asked people round / why –
AIMEE	you don't know no people to / ask.
ELAYNE	why are they comin round? Uninvited.
DEVON	She don't know / no one.
ELAYNE	Don't need no bell cos if you ent invited don't come and if you do come and I'm out –
AIMEE	you don't go / out.
ELAYNE	leave a note. Simple. *Simple shit.*
	Beat.
	And I never did go no Woolworths cos it was a shit shop from the get go.
DEVON	When you have company –
ELAYNE	I don't want / company.
AIMEE	She don't want company –
ELAYNE	don't speak for / me.
DEVON	When company comes –
ELAYNE	don't want no company.
DEVON	When company / comes –
AIMEE	Who's gonna wanna come by her?
ELAYNE	I don't need no / company.

DEVON	When company's standing on your doorstep confused… don't come to me, cos that shit looks bad on you, thass all I'm sayin. Whole heapa shit could be avoided by a bell that works – but who am I?
AIMEE	(*dry*) Yeh who are / yer?
DEVON	Who the fuck am I to say anything – who the fuck am I to know?
ELAYNE	…I do know people. I do go / out.
AIMEE	You don't.
DEVON	Woolworths was alright, y'know
ELAYNE	I do
AIMEE	you don't.
DEVON	…Their pick and mix was on point.

Scene Three

> ELAYNE*'s place as before.*
>
> TREY *sits with them, quietly sings to himself at times. It irritates* DEVON *who tries to ignore it.*
>
> *Beat.*

DEVON	You can't write your own.
AIMEE	Exactly.
DEVON	Writing your own is wrong.
ELAYNE	Who / asked – ?
AIMEE	'Arrogant'
DEVON	Arrogant.

ELAYNE	Who asked your opinion?
DEVON	A eulogy is a –
AIMEE	I tried to tell her
DEVON	a eulogy is meant to be written / by –
AIMEE	I tried / tellin –
DEVON	and you (AIMEE) never said nuthin?
AIMEE	Me sayin somethin weren't appreciated –
ELAYNE	cos it was shit.
DEVON	People'll be like –
AIMEE	thass what I said.
DEVON	They'll say things like –
AIMEE	thass what I said – she'll be the first to go anyway.
ELAYNE	Fuck / off.
DEVON	You got plans? She got plans / to – ?
ELAYNE	I don't got no plans to – fuck / off.
AIMEE	She'll be first though –
ELAYNE	aint got no plans to do nuthin stupid
AIMEE	it's not stupid. Goin first is admirable.
ELAYNE	
AIMEE	I'd admire y'for it. You're that type.
DEVON	There's something about it.
ELAYNE	Right.
AIMEE	There is something about it
DEVON	there is
AIMEE	most everybody aint got the bottle to do it. Somethin brave about those that do, if you ask me.

ELAYNE	No one's askin you.
DEVON	Now you've pissed her off.
ELAYNE	Who's askin you?
DEVON	She piss you / off?
ELAYNE	(I) aint doin shit – ent got no plans to do that shit, you do you if you want something to do.
AIMEE	I didn't piss her / off.
DEVON	She's pissed off.
AIMEE	And I'm not lookin for something to do, I was just bein nice and sayin / that –
ELAYNE	I'm not pissed off.
DEVON	She is irritatin –
ELAYNE	I'm not pissed / off.
DEVON	you're pissed off
AIMEE	(I) didn't say nuthin.
ELAYNE	I'm –
DEVON	she's pissed / off.
AIMEE	Don't speak for her.
DEVON	(*to* AIMEE) You've pissed her off – (*to* ELAYNE) (I) know she's annoyin –
AIMEE	how am I / annoyin?
DEVON	but you shouldn't / let –
AIMEE	Am I / annoying?
DEVON	that part about her piss you off.
ELAYNE	I'm not pissed off.
AIMEE	I only said / that –
DEVON	(She) annoys me.
AIMEE	I don't.

DEVON	Grates.
AIMEE	Devon –
DEVON	juss ride it – ignore it – ignore / her.
AIMEE	Am I annoyin am I annoyin?
DEVON	This singing's annoyin.
ELAYNE	It's nice.
AIMEE	Am I (annoyin) see – no I am / not.
DEVON	*Thass* something that's / annoying.
AIMEE	I am not.
DEVON	Touch of a tune hidin in there somewhere struggling to come out –
ELAYNE	leave / him.
DEVON	what you actually singin?
ELAYNE	Leave him alone.
DEVON	…I'd have singin at mine –
AIMEE	tacky
DEVON	a live singer an' that – a choir – two –
AIMEE	tack
DEVON	but not this one strangling whatever's straining to come out.
AIMEE	A funeral or a concert? What's yours meant to be? You don't know what yours is meant / to be.
ELAYNE	He wouldn't sing at yours.
DEVON	He can't sing.
ELAYNE	He's too good to sing at yours – I'd tell him not to sing at yours
DEVON	and you can't sing nuthin neither –

AIMEE   whatchu gonna do sell CDs? Sell tickets and
               CDs of your service – concert – funeral or
               whatever-the-fuck it is.

DEVON   Her (AIMEE's) singin be as annoyin as her
               talkin and I'd bury this one (TREY) in the
               back row to blend in while the rest a the
               voices do the best of the / rest.

ELAYNE   He can still hear you.

DEVON   (to AIMEE) You wouldn't be at mine

ELAYNE   he's not deaf

DEVON   tone deaf.

AIMEE   I wouldn't wanna come to your concert-
               funeral whatever-the-fuck.

ELAYNE   He sings beautiful –

DEVON   you (AIMEE) be gagging to get in – get
               security to lock you out.

AIMEE   What, you borrowing her security are yer?

DEVON   And the last person on God's green earth I'd
               ask to sing at mine –

AIMEE   (I'm) not comin to yours

DEVON   (re: AIMEE) would be you anyway. (re:
               TREY) After him.

               Beat.

ELAYNE   …(I'd) have food after mine. Loads.

AIMEE   …I'd do –

DEVON   (to AIMEE) wouldn't eat your food.

AIMEE   I'd / have –

DEVON   nah.

AIMEE   I'd / do –

DEVON	You aint even thought about it – she aint even thought about / it.
AIMEE	I'd have –
DEVON	soft crisps.
AIMEE	I'd –
ELAYNE	Wotsits.
DEVON	Nuthin to eat no choir what kinda fucked up finale – (I) definitely aint attending.
ELAYNE	Rude to say no, you'd be on the invite list.
AIMEE	No he wouldn't –
ELAYNE	he would if I'm doin it.
AIMEE	You'da took yourself by then –
ELAYNE	I wouldn't –
AIMEE	long gone
ELAYNE	no
AIMEE	and I would do food… I would do somethin…
	ELAYNE *and* DEVON *aren't convinced.*
DEVON	*I'd* have a spread. Propah. Cook up.
ELAYNE	You don't cook.
DEVON	Don't need to, be plenty of offers. Leave instructions before I go. Legal like. Un-fuck-upable.
ELAYNE	A list.
DEVON	Yeh a list.
ELAYNE	See.
AIMEE	I wouldn't cook at yours.
DEVON	Instructions be written for you not to cook – legal.
ELAYNE	Type it cos she can't read

AIMEE   *can* read just not your shit scribbles.

DEVON   And your cooking's crap (AIMEE) and you're not invited – security's already shut you out, see? Have a old skool spread hot and cold, afternoon and evening, something uplifting sung thru'out – not by him (TREY) – send me off propah. And not no finger-picking-no-vibe-ting that you'd have.

ELAYNE   She'd have bring-a-dish –

DEVON   bring your own, pick your own and drink a bottle of what you bring an' all. Rubbish.

ELAYNE *and* DEVON *laugh.*

AIMEE   …I'm goin by natural causes.

DEVON   You hope. Somebody'd do you something with your loud mouth before nature could get to you to take iss natural course.

AIMEE   She's not.

ELAYNE   Y'don't know nuthin bout how I'd go –

AIMEE   (I'm) not havin a dig – I'm not havin a / –

DEVON   aren't yer?

AIMEE   Not havin a pop –

ELAYNE   she is

AIMEE   just – y'know –

ELAYNE   you are

AIMEE   I'm not. Elayne.

ELAYNE
AIMEE

AIMEE   …I dunno. I'm just – look – . Pills or something mixed with somethin – that might work for you

ELAYNE   don't drink like you do.

AIMEE	Cos you're good like that. Do it sober then. See, if you was gonna do this you'd be the type to get it right, aint it Devon? Get it right first time and I know you're pissed off –
ELAYNE	you don't know I'm pissed / off
AIMEE	you're there all pissed / off
ELAYNE	I'm not pissed off
AIMEE	I'm just sayin that someone like me'd mess it up an' do something wrong end up more frigged than I already am. But you're… meticulous like that. Wouldn't get it wrong where I would, that's all I'm…
ELAYNE	
AIMEE	Look how you don't drink –
ELAYNE	don't drink like you.
AIMEE	See what I mean. Disciplined. I don't even drink much – but you. She's… isn't it? Devon.
ELAYNE	
AIMEE	Somethin… fearless bout you. It's good. I aint got that. Toldju. Somethin to admire. It's… admirable.

Beat.

ELAYNE	…I wouldn't do pills –
AIMEE	pills is painless. There's somethin generous about it – if you think about it. Like… it's not waitin for no one or nuthin else. It's not drama. It's sure. You're sure. You're that type a person –
ELAYNE	no I'm / not.
AIMEE	it's private. Unimposin.

ELAYNE

AIMEE   You're that type of person.

ELAYNE

AIMEE   I aint got what you got about you, I couldn't
               do it. Couldn't do what you could, what you
               would. Will. What you got about you is
               better'n what I got about me. A little bit,
               brilliant. In that respect. Thass sayin
               something.

               Beat.

DEVON   … I'd go out how I live life –

AIMEE   infringing on others, something messy that
               somebody else has gotta clear up.

DEVON   Somethin dramatic.

AIMEE
ELAYNE

DEVON   Be something their fault. (I'd) be goin about
               my business when someone would get their
               something wrong, end up in my innocent
               demise but bein *their* fault. Thass how'd /
               I'd go.

AIMEE   You'd be blameless?

DEVON   I am blameless.

AIMEE   Be out buying a bell or something, carrying it
               back and get mown down… by a bus not even
               a car – a bendy bus.

DEVON   Bendy buses have done.

AIMEE   One would still find / you.

DEVON   And the reason I'd be out bell buying would
               be cos she ent fixed her shit and don't go out
               to get nuthin to fix it, so my demise would
               rest squarely on your shoulders and on your
               conscience and it wouldn't be no bendy bus
               it would be some-some-

AIMEE	cyclist or something – nuthin glamorous about / it.
DEVON	fuck off. Some-some-like-like a power car or something – a sports car gone outta control – owner out of they depth think they handling it but don't, can't – lose it for a moment and…
DEVON AIMEE	
DEVON	Some good-shit-something like that. Tragic.
AIMEE	…Who d'you know driving round here something like that? (*to* ELAYNE) You know anyone with wheels like that?
DEVON	Don't ask her she don't know no one with wheels like / that –
AIMEE	*I* don't know no one / with –
DEVON	you don't know them kinda peoples and she don't know no one else, she don't know nuthin.
ELAYNE	Least I'd be missed.
DEVON	When you know people – speak yeh?
ELAYNE	When you stop speakin shit and shut up then I'll be quiet.
ELAYNE DEVON	
DEVON	…Mine'd be a freak accident.
AIMEE	Your fault.
DEVON	Freak accident. Act of God.
ELAYNE	(A) good Act of God.
DEVON	Piss / off.
AIMEE	In a supercar.

DEVON	Piss off.
ELAYNE	Outside Woolworths.
DEVON	Get your shit bell fixed you can rest easy / knowing –
ELAYNE	I rest / easy.
DEVON	knowing it's not your fault –
ELAYNE	iss not my / fault
DEVON	and you're not to blame.
AIMEE	Iss not her fault
ELAYNE	it's not my / fault.
AIMEE	It's not your fault.
ELAYNE	I rest easy.
DEVON	Leave it as it is and you'll be left wondering. Anyhow… Thass how I'd go out.

Beat.
There is a silence.

ELAYNE	…I wouldn't feel guilty if my bell was the cause a your –
DEVON	yeh you would.

Beat.

ELAYNE	I wouldn't feel guilty if –
DEVON	you would.

Beat.

ELAYNE	I wouldn't.
DEVON	
ELAYNE	I wouldn't give a shit.
ELAYNE DEVON	

Pause.

ELAYNE   …I'd have food / at my –

DEVON   Not as good as mine.

                AIMEE *watches them.*

ELAYNE   I'd have –

DEVON   not as much as mine.

ELAYNE
DEVON
ELAYNE
DEVON

                ELAYNE *is the first to break.*

DEVON   If you want any help goin first, you just say,
                yeh?

ELAYNE
ELAYNE

                DEVON *lights up a cigarette.*
                Beat.
                TREY *continues to sing.*
                Beat.
                Beat.
                TREY *stops singing.*

TREY   (*quietly, re: DEVON*) I wouldn't sing at
                your funeral and I'd shake the hand of the
                supercar driver… and I'm not deaf or tone
                deaf neither.

                And the bell aint broke. And it would be your
                fault. And she don't like smoking in here.

                DEVON *smokes.*

                It's a liability for my larynx havin your toxins
                airborne.

DEVON   (*dry*) Whoo.

                DEVON *watches him, smokes.*

TREY

Just you bein, is damagin.

Beat.
DEVON *smokes.*

And I'd sing a su'un till my last breath, sing su'un sweet with my last breath.

Go out on a note. That'd be me.

And there wouldn't be no crowd and wouldn't be no security and wouldn't be no whole heap, just a true two or three sincere and close and paying attention paying their respects is all / I'd ask.

DEVON

Not interested and nobody's askin.

TREY

You wouldn't be there.

ELAYNE

I'm askin.

TREY

…You would but he wouldn't and you wouldn't –

AIMEE

I wouldn't come.

TREY

(*to* ELAYNE) And you shouldn't do it Elayne, whatever they say.

ELAYNE

There is no ashtray. AIMEE *and* ELAYNE *watch as* DEVON *slowly flicks his ash into his palm.*
DEVON *continues to smoke, continues to ash it into his hand.* AIMEE *watches, curious. He smokes, gestures for her to hold out her hand.*

AIMEE

Fuck off.

DEVON *smokes.* TREY *watches him.*

DEVON

Ent illegal to smoke indoors.

ELAYNE

Ent your house.

DEVON	Ent the point.
TREY	Isn't your house.

DEVON *ashes into his hand ignoring* TREY *and watching* AIMEE *as he smokes. Tentatively* AIMEE *holds out her hand – then bottles it.*

DEVON *gently puts his ash from his hand into hers.*

AIMEE	It don't hurt?

DEVON *smokes gently holding* AIMEE's *hand, he watches her intently as he upturns her palm and gently flicks hot ash from the cigarette into it. She flinches but takes it.* AIMEE *giggles,* DEVON *shrugs,* TREY *restarts singing.*

ELAYNE	No
AIMEE	I done it – try it.
ELAYNE	
AIMEE	It don't / hurt.
ELAYNE	I don't wanna try / it.
DEVON	Party trick.
ELAYNE	This aint no party.
DEVON	She don't have / parties.
AIMEE	Try it.
DEVON	Leave / her.
ELAYNE	I don't / wanna.
AIMEE	Whassamatter with / you?
DEVON	She ent like that, leave her.
ELAYNE	Ent like what?

DEVON *smiles, says nothing.*

What?

DEVON *is quietly amused.*

DEVON	You ent the tryin kind.
ELAYNE	
AIMEE	Come 'ere come 'ere gimme your hand – spark me up –
DEVON	you don't smoke
AIMEE	no more – still got a stash little one ent gonna get me restarted you spark it up I just wanna / show her.
DEVON	How can you smoke them?
ELAYNE	I'm / not –
AIMEE	How can you smoke *them*?
ELAYNE	I'm not doin it
DEVON	(they're) cheaper
ELAYNE	(I'm) not gonna do / it.
AIMEE	I aint cheap.
DEVON	Really?
AIMEE	Spark me up c'mon –

TREY *isn't impressed.*

DEVON	(*to* TREY) whatchu lookin at?

TREY *exits.* DEVON *lights* AIMEE*'s cigarette.*

AIMEE	Gimme your hand gimme your / hand –
ELAYNE	No, no.
AIMEE	Come on –
ELAYNE	no
AIMEE	c'mon just –
ELAYNE	don't

AIMEE	Elayne, I'm not gonna hurt / you.
ELAYNE	don't
AIMEE	c'mon
DEVON	she don't wanna do it.

AIMEE gently pulls ELAYNE's hand towards her, she gently blows on the cigarette tip again, speeding up the burning of the ash.

Gently AIMEE flicks the ash into the reluctant, flinching palm of ELAYNE.

It doesn't hurt.

AIMEE	See.

AIMEE flicks the ash again into ELAYNE's palm.

Toldja.

Beat.

AIMEE slowly takes another pull from the cigarette. She watches ELAYNE.
Beat.
AIMEE slowly lowers the cigarette closer and closer to ELAYNE's skin.

D'you dare me?

AIMEE lowers the cigarette closer to ELAYNE's skin.

DEVON	Aimee.
AIMEE	(*to* ELAYNE) Do yer?
ELAYNE	
AIMEE	…Dare yer to dare me.

AIMEE lowers the cigarette even closer to ELAYNE's skin.

…Dare yer – .

*There is the sound of knocking from outside
the front door.
Surprised, they wait listening.
Beat.
The crackle of the weak bell.*

ACT TWO

Scene One

        EX-WIFE*'s place*, EX-HUSBAND *is there.*

        He drinks from a hot drink provided by
        EX-WIFE.

EX-WIFE   Wednesdays.
                     Wednesdays –

EX-HUSBAND   'Wednesdays'?

EX-WIFE   Wednesdays when you take her –

EX-HUSBAND   I don't 'take' / her.

EX-WIFE   When you have her.

EX-HUSBAND   S'not takin. Say I'm takin – sayin / I'm
                     taking –

EX-WIFE   You know / what –

EX-HUSBAND   'takin's' like stealin –

EX-WIFE   know what / I mean.

EX-HUSBAND   'taking's' not havin something in the first place
                     takin shit away from A so B goddit instead –

EX-WIFE   thass / what –

EX-HUSBAND   'takin' what ent / mine

EX-WIFE   thass what / it –

EX-HUSBAND   I don't 'take' nuthin I don't 'steal' nuthin –
                     Maya ent nuthin to 'have'. I ent no – you
                     need to say whatchu mean cos nah I don't
                     know 'what you meanin' don't know whatchu
                     doin by not sayin what you mean tho you
                     seem to be sayin your cryptic shit deliberate.
                     She's not 'taken'.

EX-WIFE   She's not with me.

EX-HUSBAND   Which don't mean shit. You say this shit –
                         you drop shit out there see where it lands
                         don't say nuthin sit back and see what / it do.

EX-WIFE   When Maya's not with / me –

EX-HUSBAND   This is how / you –

EX-WIFE   when she's not / with me it –

EX-HUSBAND   this is how you do you don't change but –

EX-WIFE   I don't change?

EX-HUSBAND   But your shit don't work on me no more –

EX-WIFE   I'm consistent

EX-HUSBAND   stuck

EX-WIFE   reliable which is something you wanna / try.

EX-HUSBAND   *Stuck.*

                         Beat.

                         And when she's not with you –

EX-WIFE   she's not with me

EX-HUSBAND   she's with me spending time, having time –
                         on our days – on our every other weekend
                         and agreed arranged day which is our
                         Wednesdays –

EX-WIFE   when you take her.

EX-HUSBAND   When... I 'have' her and when we spend time
                         an' when I bring her back happier'n when
                         she left.

EX-WIFE   You know what state she comes back / in.

EX-HUSBAND   I know what state me and she partin on,
                         happy and laughin and carefree dunno what
                         moodshift she have to mek when she steps
                         back in here with you – what mood you put
                         her in –

EX-WIFE   I don't / put her –

EX-HUSBAND   nah 'I don't know that'. Steppin in here would fuck me off.

EX-WIFE   I don't put her in no mood she ent already feelin for herself.

EX-HUSBAND   Did fuck me off. You gotta talent a fuckin off the most mellow of moods.

EX-WIFE   Her smilin and laughing and whatever the frig you think she doin with you – in fronta you – she can drop when she steps back in with me cos she knows she can be herself –

EX-HUSBAND   she is / herself.

EX-WIFE   ent under the enjoyment police you been puttin on her / all day.

EX-HUSBAND   Freer with me, happier on our Wednesdays than she is in your rest of the week.

EX-WIFE   Says the one day a weeker –

EX-HUSBAND   quality not quantity –

EX-WIFE   says the one day a / weeker.

EX-HUSBAND   that shit don't matter

EX-WIFE   says the Wednesday dad.

EX-HUSBAND   That shit don't / matter.

EX-WIFE   To the full time mum – fuck off – you / don't –

EX-HUSBAND   Cussin me / now?

EX-WIFE   you don't even know her – she shows you what she wants to show for one / day.

EX-HUSBAND   I don't know her?

EX-WIFE   *Knows* how to show what she wants to show you for one day – not even a day – *daylight / hours*.

EX-HUSBAND   I don't know / her?

EX-WIFE   Musta learnt how to maintain from me, me havin to maintain for years with *you* and you / drop her –

EX-HUSBAND   'I don't know / her.'

EX-WIFE   you drop her back thinkin you / know.

EX-HUSBAND   'Maintaining' with me?

EX-WIFE   Thinkin you know it all –

EX-HUSBAND   she knows I know / her.

EX-WIFE   thinking you know it all when you don't know nuthin don't know nuthin bout her – don't know nuthin bout her worth knowin.

EX-HUSBAND   Everythin about her's worth knowin – see – difference between me and you, you ignore, I pay attention

EX-WIFE   difference between you and me couldn't be more different – I do it. You play at it. And I won't / take –

EX-HUSBAND   Quality not / quantity.

EX-WIFE   I won't take no parenting tips from a part time parent – andju don't know what you're droppin her back to, how she lives how we live lovely – nicely. You don't know that but somehow you're still talkin – your same old shitness still shining through.

EX-HUSBAND   (*dry*) Consistent.

EX-WIFE   Consistently shit. Consistently shit years of bein with you –

EX-HUSBAND   you're not with me.

EX-WIFE   I'm not with you. No more.

               Beat.

EX-HUSBAND   And. 'Years a shit'?

EX-WIFE   Years a / shit.

EX-HUSBAND   Best years you ever had.
               I was your respite.

EX-WIFE   You were my problem.

EX-HUSBAND   I weren't your problem. I was who you brought
               your fucked up family problems back to.

EX-WIFE   You were a / problem.

EX-HUSBAND   You know I weren't and I woulda been a nice
               problem to have. To have kept.

EX-WIFE

EX-HUSBAND   You was a nice problem to have. For a /
               minute.

EX-WIFE   You could look after yourself.

EX-HUSBAND   I could look after myself.

EX-WIFE   Well / then.

EX-HUSBAND   I wanted to look after you.

EX-WIFE   I'm not goin / over –

EX-HUSBAND   I'm not bringin / up –

EX-WIFE   I'm not goin over all that –

EX-HUSBAND   shit

EX-WIFE   again.

EX-HUSBAND   Nah.

EX-WIFE   Nah.

BOTH   Nah.

               Beat.

EX-HUSBAND   …She comin?

EX-WIFE

EX-HUSBAND   Me and her is alike.

EX-WIFE   …You're not.

EX-HUSBAND   Maya tells me we're alike.

Ex WFE   She don't.

EX-HUSBAND   Tells me that I can read her, that I know her better'n you do.

EX-WIFE   She doesn't / say –

EX-HUSBAND   You don't know what she / says.

EX-WIFE   She wouldn't say that and she's not like you.

EX-HUSBAND   She's not like / you.

EX-WIFE   No one's like you – don't need no other you – another / you.

EX-HUSBAND   She got my eyes.

EX-WIFE   Nope.

EX-HUSBAND   She got my face / shape.

EX-WIFE   She ent inherited none a you, nuthin from you –

EX-HUSBAND   she's gettin my / stance.

EX-WIFE   not a look not a gesture not nuthin no she hasn't.

Beat.

EX-HUSBAND   Got my mouth –

EX-WIFE   not the shit that comes outta it. Not her way of thinkin – she *got* a way of thinkin, so not like you there – she got a way of thinking that meks *sense* so *definitely* not a piece a you there all her good shit she gets from me, my side –

EX-HUSBAND   your side?

EX-WIFE   From *me*.

EX-HUSBAND   (She) needs nuthin from your fuckin / side.

EX-WIFE   And any of her faults are either your frig-up bits tryinta infiltrate or some anomaly that her genetics is still tryin to shake out from you.

EX-HUSBAND   'Anomaly'?

EX-WIFE   'Anomaly.'

EX-HUSBAND   You need to stop watchin Countdown

EX-WIFE   go read a fuckin book.

EX-HUSBAND

EX-WIFE   She ent like you. She's better.

Beat.

EX-HUSBAND   You ent got no idea what she sayin. Bout you…

EX-WIFE
EX-HUSBAND

EX-HUSBAND   …Have you?

EX-WIFE
EX-HUSBAND

EX-WIFE   (*quietly*) …Fuck off.

EX-HUSBAND   …Cos you still don't lissen.
Still won't lissen. Still the same. 'Consistent.'
You got ignorance down to a fine art.

EX-WIFE   Had a good teacher.

EX-HUSBAND   When you 'take' her back –

EX-WIFE   it's not 'taking' back – she's 'coming' home.

EX-HUSBAND   Whatever mood she's in with you is the mood
you put her in. Cos the good times we have,
are only shitted on by the limited time
allowed before she has to come back here for
her endless days a livin. With you. We both
got shit to say bout that –

EX-WIFE   don't drag her / into –

EX-HUSBAND   both gotta lot to say bout / that.

EX-WIFE   why are you draggin her into your bitterness?

EX-HUSBAND   She's already there with her own, like bein on a leash –

EX-WIFE   which you need.

EX-HUSBAND   'Like bein on a twelve-hour leash' she says

EX-WIFE   no she don't

EX-HUSBAND   which she don't like feelin, don't like me feelin, don't like seein me feel that.

EX-WIFE

EX-HUSBAND

EX-HUSBAND   However much I try to mask it.
I don't wanna drag her in – try not to drag her in… But she ent stupid. She got a lot to say.

EX-WIFE

EX-HUSBAND   She speaks her mind, like / me.

EX-WIFE   She can read you cos you easy to read. Y'like a blank page or a page writ by a five year old –

EX-HUSBAND   she –

EX-WIFE   with two words: 'Fucked. Up' written / on.

EX-HUSBAND   Fucked up by you.

EX-WIFE   Nu'un deep about yer – you don't try to mask nuthin and she'll be lookin for layers and realise there's only one –

EX-HUSBAND   don't

EX-WIFE   like I did – try to go deep with yer and see iss juss shallow – like I did –

EX-HUSBAND   don't

EX-WIFE   years a that – boring. Nuthin to yer – borin.

EX-HUSBAND   You didn't / get –

EX-WIFE   It gets borin *you* get borin you *were* borin it was borin. All of it.

EX-HUSBAND   …All of it?

EX-WIFE   All of it.

Beat.

EX-HUSBAND   Better to be a blank page than a closed book.

Beat.

EX-WIFE   Book a parenting page one –

EX-HUSBAND   she knows you don't wanna hear, knows what you don't wanna / hear.

EX-WIFE   'Don't Drag the Kid into Your Shit.' Page one – you wouldn't have read that –

EX-HUSBAND   don't need no parenting book – (I) didn't need no parenting book – didn't have to look up what comes naturally did I? Not knowin how to be a mother is backward.

EX-WIFE   I knew how – I know / how.

EX-HUSBAND   Fucking –

EX-WIFE   advice ent / a –

EX-HUSBAND   no instincts

EX-WIFE   getting advice ent a / problem.

EX-HUSBAND   nuthin natural.

EX-WIFE   And what I naturally got is a good thing, (I) just wanted to enhance – to double check seein as I weren't getting no support from you.

EX-HUSBAND   I'm there bein a dad, while you still workin out what bein a mum is

EX-WIFE   I was depressed

EX-HUSBAND   you're depressing.

EX-WIFE   I was goin through something

EX-HUSBAND   you always were. You attract it. You're attracted to it. You love it. Love the fuckin drama – I didn't have time to be fuckin

depressed – I wish, and Maya knows you
don't wanna hear how limited she feels our
time is together so she don't say nuthin, learnt
to not say nuthin to you. I know how she feels.
History repeatin – know how she fuckin feels.
Not being able to express herself. With you.

You wanna be in everyone else's drama –

EX-WIFE	s'not 'everyone' / else's.
EX-HUSBAND	thass up to you – but she needs –
EX-WIFE	she got everythin she needs.
EX-HUSBAND	She wants –
EX-WIFE	she got everythin she needs.
EX-HUSBAND	You're startin to be like –
EX-WIFE	*what?*
EX-HUSBAND	Startin to sound like –
EX-WIFE	*what?*
EX-HUSBAND	
EX-WIFE	Sound like who…?
EX-HUSBAND	
EX-WIFE	…This is why –
EX-HUSBAND	'this is why' what?
EX-WIFE	This –
EX-HUSBAND	what?

Pause.

EX-WIFE	…She's a bath baby. Like me. *Like me.* Gets that from me.
EX-HUSBAND	She likes –
EX-WIFE	she *loves* a bath.
EX-HUSBAND	Showers at mine.
EX-WIFE	(She) don't need to shower at / yours.

EX-HUSBAND   Power shower-large-headed-temperature-controlled-tropical-setting hi-spec piece a tech something – on Wednesdays, she's in it for hours, singin / away.

EX-WIFE   She don't / sing.

EX-HUSBAND   Showering till she can't shower no more.

EX-WIFE   She don't / sing.

EX-HUSBAND   Rinsing out my hot water – ringin out at the top of her voice – and she do sing she just don't sing here. Wid you.

Tho't you woulda known that. How she sing so.

Knowin her how you do.

Old skool. She know all my old skool somethins, singin em thru to the point I have to tell her to shut up – we only in the car two minutes on our way to start our Wednesday and she already started. Happy an' carefree – starts off wid a hum along, escalates into a tune till she burstin into song proper. Iss a niceness but it do get on your nerves after a while when you can't hear who should be singing it singin it, cos she's expressin herself so loud. Beautiful, but.

…What she sing when she's wid you?

When she's 'home' with you?

When you 'have' her. What she sing then?

Beat.

EX-WIFE   She don't need no shower from she leaves here after havin a bath.

EX-HUSBAND   …Showering to scrub off the shit she's leaving here / with.

EX-WIFE   She got nuthin to scrub off – this place is spotless.

EX-HUSBAND   Clinical.

EX-WIFE   Clean.

EX-HUSBAND   Weren't talkin bout the place.

EX-WIFE   You tryinta get deep?

EX-HUSBAND

EX-WIFE   (*dry*) Don't.

EX-HUSBAND   And I was always fresh. Always did hold a fresh. Always did smell good how you did like… How you do like.

EX-WIFE
EX-HUSBAND

EX-HUSBAND   …Get a shower.
Get a – Maya'd love / it.

EX-WIFE   Showers are shit.

EX-HUSBAND   S'not about / you.

EX-WIFE   (A) few drops of water not washin you right? No.

EX-HUSBAND   You liked showerin with me.

EX-WIFE

EX-HUSBAND   Get a shower.

EX-WIFE   Don't say what I should be / doin.

EX-HUSBAND   Ent tellin you / what –

EX-WIFE   Tellin me what I should be doin – sort your own shit / out.

EX-HUSBAND   Not tellin you what to do just sayin she would / love a –

EX-WIFE   Like you know best – when did you ever know / best?

EX-HUSBAND   I was best for you.

EX-WIFE   (Don't) sit there and tell me anything –

EX-HUSBAND   I was best for / you.

EX-WIFE   don't sit there and tell me / nuthin.

EX-HUSBAND   You needed tellin something – you need tellin / something.

EX-WIFE   That wouldn't be from you those days is over.

EX-HUSBAND   Save my breath for somethin else for someone else.

EX-WIFE   Someone else?

EX-HUSBAND   Someone else.

EX-WIFE   …Like who?

EX-WIFE
EX-HUSBAND

EX-WIFE   Like who?

EX-HUSBAND

EX-HUSBAND   You askin?

EX-WIFE   I'm askin.

EX-HUSBAND   You're askin askin or – ?

EX-WIFE   I'm…

EX-HUSBAND

EX-WIFE   … No. I'm not.

Beat.

EX-HUSBAND   …She'd love a shower in here. Thass all I'm sayin – *suggestin*.
Her.
Then maybe you'd hear her sing.

EX-WIFE   …Your music was my music.

EX-HUSBAND   I came with my own / shit.

EX-WIFE   Your taste in music was – you had to be taught / taste.

EX-HUSBAND   I came with my own good shit.

EX-WIFE   Got influenced by / my –

EX-HUSBAND   Any shift in taste shoulda been taught bout my taste in woman.

EX-WIFE   Taste in woman was all you had. My taste in man was fuckin dreadful. And anythin she's singing is sung from something you woulda got from me. Anything she's singing that sounds good woulda come / from –

EX-HUSBAND   She makes everything sound good.

EX-WIFE

EX-HUSBAND   She can sing the phone book and find a melody in it – don't know the words an' she'll make em up make something up – sing about anything – sing about singing – sing about me (when) she run outta things to sing…

EX-WIFE

EX-HUSBAND   Funny shit.

EX-WIFE
EX-HUSBAND

EX-HUSBAND   (She) sings bout you to me.

EX-WIFE   No she don't.

EX-HUSBAND   …Makes up little / rhymes.

EX-WIFE   No she don't.

              EX-HUSBAND *lights up, looks at his watch, smokes.*

EX-HUSBAND   Makes me learn them.

EX-WIFE
EX-HUSBAND

EX-HUSBAND   (*dry*) …She don't then.

              Beat.

EX-WIFE   You lighting up?

EX-HUSBAND Nope.

He smokes.

EX-WIFE You smoking in fronta me?

EX-HUSBAND Nope.

He exhales a trail of smoke towards her.

EX-WIFE Smokers.

EX-HUSBAND Says the ex-smoker.

He smokes.

EX-WIFE Smokers smoking in fronta me, on a Wednesday.

EX-HUSBAND If you truly given up you wouldn't even wannit.

EX-WIFE Don't wannit.

She watches him smoke.

Shouldn't be sittin temptin me –

EX-HUSBAND shouldn't be able to be tempted.

EX-HUSBAND *exhales his smoke in her direction again.*

EX-WIFE Only thing you could tempt me wid.

EX-HUSBAND Really.

EX-WIFE Really.

EX-HUSBAND Had somethin

EX-WIFE for a minute. Thirteen years a – twelve and a half years a lookin for the rest.

EX-HUSBAND Thirteen years a satisfaction.
Well. Ten.

EX-WIFE …Seven.

Beat.

EX-HUSBAND …Five.

BOTH   Two.

               Beat. EX-HUSBAND *exhales his smoke long,*
               enjoys it.

EX-HUSBAND   You know you want one.

               EX-WIFE *watches him.*

               You know you want one.

               EX-WIFE *watches him.*

               You know you do…

               Beat.

               She tries to hold down a small smile.
               She doesn't hold the cigarette but takes a
               pull from his as he gently holds it temptingly
               for her.

               See… I know you.

EX-WIFE

EX-HUSBAND   I was good for you.

               He smokes.
               Beat.

               …She comin?

EX-WIFE   She's comin.

EX-HUSBAND

EX-WIFE   She's comin back.

EX-HUSBAND   From where?

EX-WIFE
EX-HUSBAND

EX-HUSBAND   I know where she is whenever she's with me.

EX-WIFE   Gone shop.

EX-HUSBAND   Where?

EX-WIFE   On her way back.

               Beat.

EX-HUSBAND	Gonna add this time on –
EX-WIFE	no you're not.
EX-HUSBAND	Gonna add this – what is *my* time / on.
EX-WIFE	No you're / not.
EX-HUSBAND	You tell her I'm comin?
EX-WIFE	She knows you're comin. She knows what day / it is.
EX-HUSBAND	You do this on purpose – I'm adding / it on.
EX-WIFE	She be back / soon.
EX-HUSBAND	We should be gone –
EX-WIFE	you drop her back late and I'm takin it off the front end of next Wednesday.
EX-HUSBAND	Then I'll drop her back later then an' all.
EX-WIFE	No you won't.
EX-HUSBAND	Drop her back when we've had our full twelve / hours.
EX-WIFE	(You'll) drop her back when she's due back. School night.
EX-HUSBAND	Drop her back when I come back if you fuck about with my schedule. (And) what kinda mother don't know where her yout' is?
EX-WIFE	I know where / she is.
EX-HUSBAND	What kinda parent is that – that on page two of your parenting books parta the chapter – 'Don't Give a Shit Where They / Are?'
EX-WIFE	(I) don't keep her under lock and chain.
EX-HUSBAND	Know where she is when she's with me –
EX-WIFE	you should do for twelve / hours.
EX-HUSBAND	she go out – I go out with her. She wanna get somewhere – I'll drive her there.
EX-WIFE	(*dry*) Sounds like fun.

EX-HUSBAND   Look and learn cos this is some kinda bullshit
and not right and not how I bring her up

EX-WIFE   you don't bring her up.

EX-HUSBAND   I bring her / up.

EX-WIFE   You *take her out*. Difference. You get the
singing I get the day in day out shit bits –

EX-HUSBAND   I'd take the day in day / out

EX-WIFE   that's 'bringin her / up'.

EX-HUSBAND   if you'd relinquish some a the hold you got /
on her.

EX-WIFE   Wouldn't change nuthin – not changing
nuthin – wouldn't change nuthin bout her cos
thass what raisin her up is. 'Beautiful. But.'

EX-HUSBAND

EX-HUSBAND   …You was a shit wife – now / you a –

EX-WIFE   A shit wife?

EX-HUSBAND   Now you showin your colours as a shit
mother.

EX-WIFE
EX-HUSBAND

EX-HUSBAND *is the first to break.*

EX-WIFE   …Them that don't know nuthin, sittin in my
yard smoking up their something and chatting
shit about things I can see is confusing
themselves, should shut their bullshit up.
Don't go deep, you'll hurt yourself. You only
a one day a weeker –

EX-HUSBAND   and you a bitch.

EX-WIFE   She's a little bit late, don't worry bout it, and
the fact you can call the mother of your child
a 'bitch' is sayin a lot about you. Y'lucky I'm
letting you sit there and wait steada standing
on the doorstep where you should be – or

sittin in your damn car, that you drive her everywhere with. Wait for her there.

EX-HUSBAND   Don't tell / me –

EX-WIFE   You bring her back late and I swear / to God –

EX-HUSBAND   don't tell me what / to do.

EX-WIFE   you will / see –

EX-HUSBAND   don't try and tell me what / to do.

EX-WIFE   see my full wrath back lashing itself round you *truss mi* – my girl (will) be back on time – I do / know that.

EX-HUSBAND   'Your girl'?

EX-WIFE   She will / be –

EX-HUSBAND   'Your girl' – fuck off.

EX-WIFE   Cos I / ent –

EX-HUSBAND   Fuck / you.

EX-WIFE   this ent no negotiation *Tyrone* – I *dun* wid negotiating yeh? This is me *telling* you – and fuck you right back.

EX-HUSBAND   Fuck you / yeh?

EX-WIFE   *Fuck you.*

EX-WIFE reaches for his cigarettes and lights up, smokes, vexed.

EX-HUSBAND   Don't take the / piss.

EX-WIFE   Don't say nothing.

She smokes.

See / why –

EX-HUSBAND   *Be* quiet.

They smoke.

See how / you –

EX-WIFE   Fuckin. Wednesdays.

                 They smoke.

EX-WIFE
EX-HUSBAND

                 Beat.
                 Beat. They smoke. A stand-off.

EX-WIFE
EX-HUSBAND

                 They smoke. They watch each other.
                 Pause
                 A key is heard in the front door lock as Maya
                 is heard making her way in. Both parents out
                 their cigarettes hurriedly, trying to waft the
                 air clean.

DAUGHTER   *(calls from offstage)* Muuum! I'm baaack! Is
                 Dad here yet?!

ACT THREE

Scene One

> EX-WIFE *is round* ELAYNE*'s place.*
> ELAYNE *has cigarette burns about her arms.*
> *Nobody else is there.*

EX-WIFE   Need to get a bell.

ELAYNE   Got a bell.

EX-WIFE   Need to get a bell that works, sick / of –

ELAYNE   Bell / works.

EX-WIFE   sick of knocking.

ELAYNE   Got a bell. You knock too quiet.

> *Beat.*

EX-WIFE   Standing outside like I'm not welcome –

ELAYNE   I heard the knock.

EX-WIFE   Confusing.

ELAYNE   I heard the / knock.

EX-WIFE   Not knowing if you heard the (knock) you heard the knock?

ELAYNE   I heard the knock.

EX-WIFE   You do this – you always do this –

ELAYNE   it's not 'always'

EX-WIFE   what was you doin?

ELAYNE   I'm doin something.

EX-WIFE   What? What normal people / do –

ELAYNE   I do / things.

EX-WIFE	normal people don't leave people lingering – y'lucky I didn't leave – y'need to get a bell and if that one ent workin and ent got no batteries –
ELAYNE	it's got batteries juss / needs –
EX-WIFE	you got money for a new one?
ELAYNE	Don't need no new / one.
EX-WIFE	You got money – got enough for cigs – got enough for batteries.
ELAYNE	Not my / cigarettes.
EX-WIFE	Don't need no name brand, them Powerzone ones ten for two pounds from Poundshop –
ELAYNE	wouldn't be two pounds from Poundshop.
EX-WIFE	Poundland then, one a them pound places do plenty batteries for a – no excuse – you got a pound for that. Know / the size?
ELAYNE	Two pounds from Poundshop get me twenty, don't need twenty, twenty batteries lying round / the place.
EX-WIFE	You know what size? Double A, triple A? You got a pound f'that – can borrow you a pound for / that.
ELAYNE	Don't need / your –
EX-WIFE	Can borrow you that to sort your battery situation.
ELAYNE	Don't need your money.
EX-WIFE	Need new batteries though don'tchu?
ELAYNE	
EX-WIFE	…I'll pick some up next time I (come). I'll put it down – write it down put it on a list – you still doin your lists? (I) won't forget but y'need to let me / know –

ELAYNE	I gotta / list.
EX-WIFE	let me know what / size.
ELAYNE	I got a list.
EX-WIFE	You got a list?
ELAYNE	I got a list.
EX-WIFE	Add em to whatever you got writ down then. Can gettem on my way round not standin outside tekkin no shame no more.
ELAYNE	And I am normal.
EX-WIFE	Never said you weren't.
ELAYNE	You said / I –
EX-WIFE	Never said you weren't –
ELAYNE	you / said –
EX-WIFE	not opening the door ent normal but from you 'opened' it, eventually… Juss not as swift with / the –
ELAYNE	You said I weren't / normal.
EX-WIFE	I didn't.
ELAYNE EX-WIFE	
EX-WIFE	I didn't.
	Beat.
ELAYNE	…Didju knock first then ring?
EX-WIFE	Rung it dunno if it was workin – knocked.
ELAYNE	Once?
EX-WIFE	What? I rung it and knocked. Then knocked louder cos I still never know if you hear it.
ELAYNE	
EX-WIFE	What?

ELAYNE	Nuthin.
EX-WIFE	What?
ELAYNE	…Maya comin?
EX-WIFE	She's not here.
ELAYNE	She comin?
EX-WIFE	Iss a Wednesday.
ELAYNE	Should bring her.
EX-WIFE	Iss a Wednesday.
ELAYNE	Can change the Wednesdays
EX-WIFE	changing anything with her dad is fuckin nuts, so –
ELAYNE	come later
EX-WIFE	later ent no good.
ELAYNE	After school –
EX-WIFE	later ent no good, she got school stuff / and –
ELAYNE	(I) like seeing her.
EX-WIFE	Y'know what they're like.
ELAYNE	She liked coming to see her old aunt
EX-WIFE	you ent that old.
ELAYNE	Older'n you
EX-WIFE	and I'm young and green still. She wouldn't like standin on your doorstep – my days she'd open her mout' –
ELAYNE	she wouldn't be standin on my doorstep.
EX-WIFE	So you'd let her in.
ELAYNE	You weren't standin on my doorstep.
EX-WIFE	
ELAYNE	Long. How's Tyrone?

EX-WIFE	Tyrone.
ELAYNE	Y'still letting him in?
EX-WIFE	Being civil.
ELAYNE	Still letting him in / then.
EX-WIFE	Bein civil – I *hear* my bell.
ELAYNE	He's still ringing something.
EX-WIFE	He's the father of my child
ELAYNE	'your' child?
EX-WIFE	Don't you / start.
ELAYNE	Most people leave their exes at the door –
EX-WIFE	'most' who – who 'most' you / know?
ELAYNE	leave them in their / car.
EX-WIFE	Who you know to 'most' / about?
ELAYNE	Bout letting them ring – letting them in. That ent really ex behaviours – he drop you round?
EX-WIFE	(We're) keepin it civil –
ELAYNE	he dropped you / round?
EX-WIFE	keepin it casual, he picks her up on a Wednesday – cool, drops her back at what o'clock on a Wednesday night – cool. Me keeping it civil like that. Adult.
ELAYNE	So you got a free ride then.
EX-WIFE	
ELAYNE	Lettin him in, first step / to –
EX-WIFE	No.
ELAYNE	Then the cup a offered hot drink –
EX-WIFE	he don't get no drink.
ELAYNE	Then the –

EX-WIFE   no – if you think –

ELAYNE   I do / think.

EX-WIFE   if you think something gonna come from /
               nuthin –

ELAYNE   I know / you.

EX-WIFE   from nuthin with that one when we – no. We
               done wid that. Got a history with that (one) I
               ent got no intention of repeating.

               …He's a arse.

               Beat.

ELAYNE   He can make you do things.

EX-WIFE   No one can make me do nuthin.

ELAYNE   Cept / him.

EX-WIFE   Nuthin that I don't wanna do. No one.
               Not no more.

ELAYNE   …Cept him.

EX-WIFE   (*dry*) …And you.
               See you still smokin.

ELAYNE   (I) don't smoke. You're my role model.

EX-WIFE   Don't start.

ELAYNE   Tyrone still sparking up?

EX-WIFE

ELAYNE   (*dry*) Not even on a Wednesday?

EX-WIFE   Where's your list?

ELAYNE

EX-WIFE   Where's / your –

ELAYNE   List ent finished.

EX-WIFE   (I) gotta get some bits

ELAYNE	gotta finish it.
EX-WIFE	Finish it and come.
ELAYNE	Got shit to do.
EX-WIFE	Come on / out.
ELAYNE	Got stuff to do in here.
EX-WIFE	Like what?
ELAYNE	
EX-WIFE	(*dry*) Cos you always so busy. Your days is so full / right?
ELAYNE	You the one always round here maybe iss you looking something to / do.
EX-WIFE	I got plenty to do.
ELAYNE	Looks like it.
EX-WIFE	(Have to) mek time to come see you
ELAYNE	don't ask it
EX-WIFE	don't have to.
ELAYNE	Don't need it
EX-WIFE	yeh y'do.
ELAYNE	Got my own shit to do
EX-WIFE	what you gotta do in here thass so urgent thatchu can't step out an' pick up two piece a batteries? 'part from clean.
ELAYNE	It is clean.
EX-WIFE	Clean clean.
ELAYNE	It is / clean.
EX-WIFE	Your version a clean –
ELAYNE	which is normal clean. Most people's clean is like / mine.

EX-WIFE   Cos *you* know how most people livin. Who
                 you been by to know? Who you know live like
                 you? A little run round with a hoover ent gonna
                 hurt, when last the hoover come out to / play?

ELAYNE   Iss been run round.

EX-WIFE   Not properly

ELAYNE   iss been done.

EX-WIFE   Little dust and bleach be a good / thing.

ELAYNE   It's been / done.

EX-WIFE   Bit a Shake n' Vac, show the floor some love –

ELAYNE   I dunnit.

EX-WIFE   When? When?

ELAYNE

EX-WIFE   Just in case ennit (*dry*) don't want company
                 comin catchin you out, keep it clean you
                 always / ready.

ELAYNE   My kinda company ent the same kinda
                 company you might have frequenting, your
                 ex's all involved –

EX-WIFE   my ex isn't 'involved' and don't frequent
                 nuthin / toldju.

ELAYNE   my kinda company ent like that

EX-WIFE   who-the-fuck-company you got? Who's here?
                 Who comes round here? Cept me and even
                 then you keep me hangin out front. Y'need to
                 put them / in.

ELAYNE   I'll put them in.

EX-WIFE   Need to sort it out – you, all inside y'yard all
                 the time –

ELAYNE   you don't know

EX-WIFE   inside here doin nuthin.

ELAYNE	You don't know
EX-WIFE	doin nuthin for days – that ent natural –
ELAYNE	y'don't / know.
EX-WIFE	that ent natural – that ent healthy – *that* ent normal there ent nuthin normal bout that. *Sis*.

Scene Two

> EX-WIFE *gently turns* ELAYNE*'s cigarette-burnt arms, concerned.* ELAYNE *pulls them away and her sleeves down, self-conscious.*
>
> AIMEE, DEVON *and* TREY *are in the room as well, but unnoticeable to* EX-WIFE.
>
> *Beat.*

ELAYNE	No.
EX-WIFE	…We here again?
ELAYNE	No.
EX-WIFE	We –
ELAYNE	no.

> *Beat.*

EX-WIFE	
EX-WIFE	You got TCP or something?
ELAYNE	TCP stinks.
EX-WIFE	TCP works.
ELAYNE	Stinks
EX-WIFE	or Savlon or somethin to / soothe it.

ELAYNE	Don't need nuthin.
EX-WIFE	Something to clean / your –
ELAYNE	They dryin out.
EX-WIFE	(You) don't wanna gettem infected.
ELAYNE	They're drying / out.
EX-WIFE	Not like before.
ELAYNE	Don't hurt – ent nuthin, not bleeding.
EX-WIFE ELAYNE	
EX-WIFE	That's something else to add to the list then.
ELAYNE	
EX-WIFE	They sore?
AIMEE	No.
ELAYNE	
EX-WIFE	They sore – look sore –
AIMEE	no.
EX-WIFE	Huh?
AIMEE	No.
ELAYNE	They're not.
EX-WIFE	…Sore before.
ELAYNE	These don't hurt.
EX-WIFE	(You) can come and buy some Savlon with the batteries –
ELAYNE	(*quietly*) don't wannit.
EX-WIFE	What?
AIMEE	Don't need it.
ELAYNE	Don't need nuthin.

EX-WIFE	(*dry*) You don't need nuthin.
AIMEE	Nuthin from her.
DEVON	(*re:* AIMEE) Be quiet.
ELAYNE	Don't need / nuthin.
EX-WIFE	'You don't need nuthin sittin there sulkin with your arms lookin like shit 'you don't need nuthin'.
AIMEE	Tell her.
DEVON	(*re:* AIMEE) Be / quiet.
ELAYNE	Not sulkin.
EX-WIFE	Looks like it.
AIMEE	She's not sulkin. (*re:* EX-WIFE) She's a bitch.
EX-WIFE	Like my name's 'fool'.
ELAYNE	
EX-WIFE	I get in the shit I don't say something.
ELAYNE	Nuthin to say.
EX-WIFE	Don't do nuthin I get in the shit.
ELAYNE	Nuthin to say nuthin to do.
EX-WIFE	You don't care about / that?
ELAYNE	Nuthin to do with you.
DEVON	Nuthin to do / with her.
EX-WIFE	(You) don't give a shit bout me or nuthin?
TREY	No.
DEVON	You're an adult Elayne.
ELAYNE	I'm an adult.
AIMEE	She don't talk to you like one –
EX-WIFE	'you're an / adult.'

AIMEE	which is saying something about her.
EX-WIFE	Really.
DEVON	You're an adult
AIMEE	she's got a problem.
EX-WIFE	Are yer?
DEVON	Hear how she's sayin it.
AIMEE	That's what I mean.
DEVON	Hear how she's sayin it
AIMEE	*she* fucks up.
ELAYNE	You fuck up.
EX-WIFE	Right.
AIMEE	*She's* allowed / to.
ELAYNE	You fuck up.
EX-WIFE	My fuck ups ent like your fuck / ups.
ELAYNE	You're allowed to –
AIMEE	she / does.
EX-WIFE	My fuck ups don't look like your arms.
ELAYNE	Your fuck ups is walking and talking eleven years later busy with 'school and stuff'.

DEVON *finds it quietly amusing.*

EX-WIFE	Maya is not a fuck up
TREY	(*to* DEVON) be / quiet
ELAYNE	'She was a mistake'
EX-WIFE	she's a blessing.
ELAYNE	You've decided.
EX-WIFE	
ELAYNE	My shit ent a fuck up neither. I've decided. I'm fine.

EX-WIFE
ELAYNE

ELAYNE   Better'n fine. I'm... brilliant.

                Beat.

EX-WIFE   You got burns on burns.

AIMEE   Nuthin deep

DEVON   not that / deep.

ELAYNE   Not burns, marks.

EX-WIFE   Elayne –

ELAYNE   not that deep.

EX-WIFE   Burns –

ELAYNE   marks

EX-WIFE   like I don't know.

ELAYNE   Don't ask then.

EX-WIFE   You a fuckin liability.

DEVON   And she's an idiot.

EX-WIFE   Do you think I'm an idiot?

AIMEE   Easy answer to that / one.

EX-WIFE   You wanna play fool you play fool but you
                aint takin me along with you – you do that
                shit I *have* to say something –

ELAYNE   I haven't *done* nuthin. I / haven't.

EX-WIFE   Your mistakes shit on me.

AIMEE   Tell her to fuck / off.

EX-WIFE   Your mistakes is involving – are involving –
                draggin me / in –

DEVON   Who asked her to come?

EX-WIFE   Draggin me / down.

AIMEE	Don't get involved.
DEVON	Who asked her to come?
AIMEE	Tell her to fuck / off.
DEVON	Don't get involved.
AIMEE	Why is she even here?
TREY	I didn't ask her.
DEVON	No one asked her to come –
ELAYNE	I never asked her to / come.
AIMEE	Did you ask her to come?
EX-WIFE	What did / you – ?
DEVON	I never asked her to / come.
ELAYNE	No one asked you to come.
AIMEE	Tell her / to –
EX-WIFE	What did you say?
DEVON	Tell her to fuck off –
ELAYNE	no.
EX-WIFE	Are / we –
AIMEE	Tell her / to –
TREY	*tell* her
ELAYNE	no.
EX-WIFE	Are we here again?
ELAYNE	
EX-WIFE	Elayne, we back here again?
ELAYNE	
EX-WIFE	Are you –
ELAYNE	I'm fine.
EX-WIFE	Are / you?

DEVON	Fuck off.
	TREY *nods*.
ELAYNE	I feel fine.
AIMEE	Fuck her / off.
EX-WIFE	You sure?
ELAYNE	We're – I am –
EX-WIFE	let me –
ELAYNE	no.
EX-WIFE	Come shops with me
ELAYNE	no.
EX-WIFE	I juss wanna –
ELAYNE/ AIMEE/DEVON	no.
EX-WIFE	Cos –
ELAYNE	I feel good –
EX-WIFE	y'don't –
TREY	I do
ELAYNE	I feel well.
EX-WIFE	Y'not –
ELAYNE	I do.
EX-WIFE	You don't.
ELAYNE	I am. …I do. I do. I'm fine.

EX-WIFE *watches* ELAYNE.

Scene Three

        EX-WIFE *and* ELAYNE *sit and smoke*
        ELAYNE*'s cigarettes.*

        Nobody else is there.

ELAYNE   You're like me.

EX-WIFE   (I'm) not like you.

        Beat.

ELAYNE   Smoke like me.

EX-WIFE   (I'm) nuthin like you.

ELAYNE   Not smoke like me but smoke like me.

EX-WIFE   I'm not like you.

ELAYNE   Know you never give up.

EX-WIFE   I've given up

ELAYNE   you can't give / up.

EX-WIFE   I've given up. This was real wouldn't be
        smoking your shit brand.

ELAYNE   I never got them.

EX-WIFE

EX-WIFE   You worry me.

ELAYNE   You worry me

EX-WIFE   my shit's alright / you –

ELAYNE   he can make you think things.

        EX-WIFE *smokes.*

EX-WIFE   …You reckon.

ELAYNE   Made you do things.

EX-WIFE *smokes*.

EX-WIFE   Who made you do what's done on your arms?

ELAYNE   Makes you not wanna come.

EX-WIFE   Who made you do / that?

ELAYNE   He made you not wanna come.

EX-WIFE   We was married

ELAYNE   which made you not wanna come.

EX-WIFE   I came.

ELAYNE   Not as much

EX-WIFE   I / came.

ELAYNE   you liked bein with him more –

EX-WIFE   we were married.

ELAYNE   He made you not wanna be here

EX-WIFE   we've done / this.

ELAYNE   he still does

EX-WIFE   no

ELAYNE   he made you not wanna / stay.

EX-WIFE   we've been over this. No he never

ELAYNE   he –

EX-WIFE   no he *never*.

ELAYNE   …You couldn't wait to get back.

EX-WIFE   What happened to your *arms* then?

ELAYNE   Made you feel like that made you do that. More'n once.

EX-WIFE *smokes*.

Made you hate Wednesdays.

EX-WIFE   I don't hate Wednesdays.

ELAYNE   Made you hate Wednesdays comin / here.

EX-WIFE   I don't hate (Wednesdays)... I don't hate
            comin here.

ELAYNE   Made you hate me.

            Beat.

EX-WIFE   (*dry*) ...I've hated you for years.

ELAYNE   ...Told him you'd still come though.

            EX-WIFE *smokes.*

            I told him I could make you do what you
            didn't wanna do more. More'n he could.

            EX-WIFE *smokes. They smoke.*

EX-WIFE   I got money in my pocket and the shop's
            round the corner. Batteries are cheap.
            Savlon's cheaper...

ELAYNE

EX-WIFE   Come out with me.

ELAYNE

EX-WIFE   Fresh air'll do you / good.

ELAYNE   Juss cos you got Maya –

EX-WIFE   (*quietly*) Jesus.
            I ent 'got' Maya. She ent nuthin to 'have'.
            Shit.

ELAYNE   You don't let her come –

EX-WIFE   she can't come, she got school –

ELAYNE   could if you wanted her to

EX-WIFE   it's a Wednesday.

ELAYNE   You could make / her.

EX-WIFE   Fuckin – she be scared seein you marked up
            like this.

ELAYNE	(I'll) wear long sleeves
EX-WIFE	(*dry*) that works.
ELAYNE	You know whatchu lookin for.
EX-WIFE	So does she.
ELAYNE	She / don't.
EX-WIFE	She does and she scared enough seein you she said she – .
ELAYNE	What?
	Beat.
EX-WIFE	…You don't know how to be around kids.
ELAYNE	You made her not wanna come.
EX-WIFE	You don't know / how to –
ELAYNE	Yes I do
EX-WIFE	you don't always geddit right.
EX-WIFE	
ELAYNE	She knows me.
EX-WIFE	She's scared a you.
ELAYNE	(Then) thass your fault.
EX-WIFE	My fault.
ELAYNE	Your bad parenting.
EX-WIFE	My bad / parentin?
ELAYNE	Your 'bad parenting'. (A) shit mum.
EX-WIFE	Nuthin to do wid you bein a fucked up aunt.
ELAYNE	Tho't you was here to save me for a minute.
EX-WIFE	You don't need savin.
ELAYNE	(You) always said I needed something.
EX-WIFE	

ELAYNE   I was just answerin her questions.

EX-WIFE   Thass my job. And if she weren't askin me,
              tell her to ask me – *thass* your / job.

ELAYNE   She wouldn't ask you

EX-WIFE   thass all you had to / do.

ELAYNE   she wouldn't ask you.

EX-WIFE   Asks me anything asks me everything, she's
              mine to tell.

ELAYNE   And you said things –

EX-WIFE   my job.

ELAYNE   Things about your '*marriage*' –

EX-WIFE   we're talking about you.

ELAYNE   You told her *nuff* things –

EX-WIFE   we're talkin bout / you.

ELAYNE   that an eleven-year-old don't need to know
              and I wanna talk about you / tho.

EX-WIFE   You've got the problem.

ELAYNE   I wanna talk about what you talked to her
              about.

EX-WIFE   You're outta order.

ELAYNE   Let's talk about that.

EX-WIFE   No.

ELAYNE   You said –

EX-WIFE   no

ELAYNE   makin her take sides –

EX-WIFE   I didn't

ELAYNE   y'know you / did.

EX-WIFE   she was watchin me and him fall apart

ELAYNE   draggin her into your shit –

EX-WIFE   she was watchin me and her / dad –

ELAYNE   proper inappropriate

EX-WIFE   was watching me and him fall / apart –

ELAYNE   you don't know how to be around your
                own kid

EX-WIFE   fall apart because of you.

                Beat.

ELAYNE   I said to her... juss said to her... that however
                shit she's feelin – bein made to feel, that
                there's always *shitter* out there.

EX-WIFE   And here you are.

ELAYNE   She's like me

EX-WIFE   she's *not* like you.

ELAYNE   Said how she loves singing –

EX-WIFE   fuck her / singing.

ELAYNE   said a lot, tells me a lot, sings when she's low
                – said she sings when / she's –

EX-WIFE   fuck / that.

ELAYNE   I sing

EX-WIFE   no you don't.

ELAYNE   We was singing –

EX-WIFE   no you weren't.

ELAYNE   Doin harmonies

EX-WIFE   no.

ELAYNE   Singing songs about you.

EX-WIFE

ELAYNE   (She) opens up to me.
                No one opens up to you.

EX-WIFE

ELAYNE   And I can't open up to her when she's
                opening up to me? I ent allowed / to?

EX-WIFE   Not like how you do.

ELAYNE   *She* can say what she wants –

EX-WIFE   she's a *kid*.

ELAYNE   *She* can say what she / wants.

EX-WIFE   *She* can say what the fuck she wants she's a /
                kid!

ELAYNE   And I can't.

EX-WIFE   You *can't*. You can't. You know that. You
                know that. Not how you do. We been over
                this… Shit. No one wants to know about
                your fuckin – *she* don't want to know bout
                your fuckin whatever-the-fuck goes on with
                you up there –

ELAYNE   you / do

EX-WIFE   freakin her out – your worries are your
                worries she don't need to know more'n she
                already / do.

ELAYNE   And what does she know?

EX-WIFE   Knows more'n enough

ELAYNE   thanks

EX-WIFE   knows I'm sick a tryinta explain shit to her
                eleven-year-old self that she don't need to
                know. Bout you. Which version a you. And if
                I did tell her details bout why me and he was
                brukin down then maybe them *details* is some
                a the reason she don't wanna come round here
                by you no more. *Sis*. She aint like you, don't
                wanna be like you, never sang wid you – is
                afraid she'll come out fucked up like you.

> EX-WIFE *kisses her teeth, frustrated.*
> ELAYNE *becomes self-conscious about her arms.*
>
> *Beat.*
> *Beat.*
>
> (*quietly*) You're doin my head in.

ELAYNE   What?

EX-WIFE   You're doin my head right in.

ELAYNE

EX-WIFE   You get like this.

ELAYNE   … (I) don't 'get' like / nuthin.

EX-WIFE   You get like this.

ELAYNE   I don't 'get' like – to 'get' somethin is to obtain / something.

EX-WIFE   Alright / alright.

ELAYNE   I ent obtained nuthin I ent already / got.

EX-WIFE   Alright alright 'getting', 'taking' fuckin hell take your fuckin meds.

> *Beat.*

ELAYNE   …I have.

> *There is a weariness about* EX-WIFE.

EX-WIFE   What happened to your arms?

ELAYNE

EX-WIFE   What happened to your arms this time?

ELAYNE

ELAYNE   …I don't / know.

EX-WIFE   Who burnt you?

ELAYNE   …I don't know.

EX-WIFE   When did / it –

ELAYNE   I don't know.

EX-WIFE   When did / you –

ELAYNE   I don't know.

EX-WIFE   When did you do it?

ELAYNE   … I don't know.

           Beat.
           Beat.

EX-WIFE   Should bathe em down in su'un.

           ELAYNE *shakes her head.*

           You got TCP or anything?

           ELAYNE *shakes her head.*

ELAYNE   Stinks.

EX-WIFE   Savlon? You got that?

           ELAYNE *shakes her head.*

           Nah. Dettol?

ELAYNE

EX-WIFE   Dettol do everythin – do the bog do the bath
           do the floors do you.

ELAYNE

EX-WIFE   No Dettol. What happened to what I bought
           you from before? Bottle dun?

ELAYNE

EX-WIFE   No Dettol then.

           Beat.
           Beat.

           They dryin up?

ELAYNE   …Scabbing over. Dryin up –

EX-WIFE   thass something.

               Pause.

               Thass something. Don't pick at em.

ELAYNE   …Not picking.

               Beat.

EX-WIFE   They hurt?

               Beat.
               ELAYNE *nods.*
               Beat.

ELAYNE   (*quietly*) …I just wanted to… I was writing
               lists.

EX-WIFE   What?

               Beat.

ELAYNE   Double A.

EX-WIFE   What?

ELAYNE   I'll put them on the list. Double A. Batteries.

EX-WIFE   You sure?

ELAYNE   I think.

ELAYNE

EX-WIFE   (I'm) not changing them if they're wrong.

               ELAYNE *sparks up a fresh cigarette.*

ELAYNE   …You seen this?

               ELAYNE *draws on her cigarette teasing the
               ash.* EX-WIFE *sighs weary.*

               You done this? Watch.

EX-WIFE

ELAYNE   Party trick – watch / this.

EX-WIFE   You don't go no parties.

ELAYNE	You / watchin?
EX-WIFE	You don't go out.

*ELAYNE holds her cigarette over her hand,
the ash hovering.*

ELAYNE	You watchin you / watchin?
EX-WIFE	Hurt your hands I ent gonna do / nuthin.
ELAYNE	Dare me to / do it?
EX-WIFE	Bu'n up y'hands I ent gonna do / nuthin.
ELAYNE	Do yer? Go on dare / me.
EX-WIFE	I ent nuthin like / you.
ELAYNE	Dare it – go on. Don't hurt (it) don't hurt – it don't (hurt) watch. *Watch.*

*ELAYNE ashes the cigarette into her hand,
smiles, continues to smoke, watching
EX-WIFE for a reaction. There is none.*

I'll show yer. It don't (hurt), gimme your...

*ELAYNE gestures for EX-WIFE's hand,
EX-WIFE doesn't respond.*

Go on, *go on,* gimme your...

*ELAYNE reaches out for EX-WIFE's hand.
EX-WIFE doesn't respond and doesn't touch
her.*

EX-WIFE
ELAYNE

*ELAYNE ashes out the cigarette slowly (not
on her hand).*

Beat.

EX-WIFE
ELAYNE

Pause.

ELAYNE   (*quietly*) …Can I hold your hand?

Please.

EX-WIFE *doesn't move.*

Beat.

…They are double A.

The size is double A. I know it. That'll fit.

I'll write it down, I've written it down.

Wilco got better ones. Not for a pound
though. More name brand if you're goin
there.

EX-WIFE *says nothing.*
Beat.
ELAYNE *gently rubs one of her arms, a bit
nervous, it's sore.*

Beat.

Slowly she starts picking at one of the scabs.

End.

A Nick Hern Book

nut first published in Great Britain in 2013 as a paperback original by Nick Hern Books Limited, Nick Hern Books Limited, The Glasshouse, 49a Goldhawk Road, London W12 8QP

nut copyright © 2013 debbie tucker green

debbie tucker green has asserted her right to be identified as the author of this work

Cover image: Joshua Miels (www.joshuamiels.com)
Cover design: Ned Hoste, 2H

Typeset by Nick Hern Books, London
Printed in Great Britain by CPI Group (UK) Ltd

A CIP catalogue record for this book is available from the British Library

ISBN 978 1 84842 335 0